Highlights

brainPLAY
HALLOWEEN
PUZZLES

BOOKS FOR PUZZLE PEOPLE

Kid tested by
Jason Hafler
Age 8
Lucy McPherson
Age 10

HIGHLIGHTS PRESS
Honesdale, Pennsylvania

ASK the
COSTUME
Quiz-inator

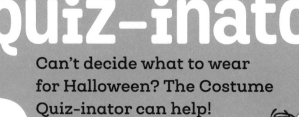

Can't decide what to wear for Halloween? The Costume Quiz-inator can help!

YOUR CLASS GETS TO HEAR A SPEAKER ON CAREER DAY. YOU HOPE IT'S

A NEW MOVIE IS COMING OUT CALLED *LITTLE RED RIDING HOOD IN SPACE!* WILL YOU GO SEE IT?

A Sounds like an adventure. I'm in!

B Sure! I always like to see creative variations on classic tales.

C What a blast! Bring on the red riding spaceships and alien wolves.

YOUR FAVORITE BOOKS ARE

A filled with action and lots of excitement!

B fantasy stories with imaginary characters.

C all types. There's no way to pick just one kind!

WHICH JACK-O'-LANTERN WOULD YOU PICK?

A   **B**   **C**

WHAT KIND OF MUSIC FITS YOU BEST?

A Dramatic music, like a movie theme song.

B Playful, magical tunes, maybe with tinkling bells or a xylophone.

C A mash-up of styles, like a rap version of "Twinkle, Twinkle, Little Star" with a burst of banjo.

WHICH WOULD YOU WANT TO WEAR?

A   **B**   **C**

WHICH SUNGLASSES WOULD YOU PICK?

A   **B**   **C**

YOU HAVE FREE TIME! WHICH DO YOU WANT TO DO?

A Film mini videos of my adventures.

B Draw kingdoms of creatures I made up myself.

C Juggle while counting in another language and standing on one foot.

If you answered mostly . . .

A Be a Hero!

Dress as a real hero, like a firefighter, or an imaginary one, like a comic-book superhero.

B Imagine That!

Go as a character from a myth or fairy tale, or invent your own creature from another world.

C Mix and Match!

Combine a bunch of ideas into a unique costume, like a rock-star dinosaur or a ballerina astronaut.

TEST YOUR EYESIGHT

WHAT IS THIS?

HINT: It's for horses!

An organ in your abdomen

A specific sequence of DNA

The chess piece that can move the most places

DO A WORD WORKOUT

Use the clues to name words that rhyme with **Halloween**.

A popular color for monster makeup

Someone between 13 and 19

BE LOGICAL

Figure out which witch's accessory should go in place of each question mark. Each column and row should contain all four items.

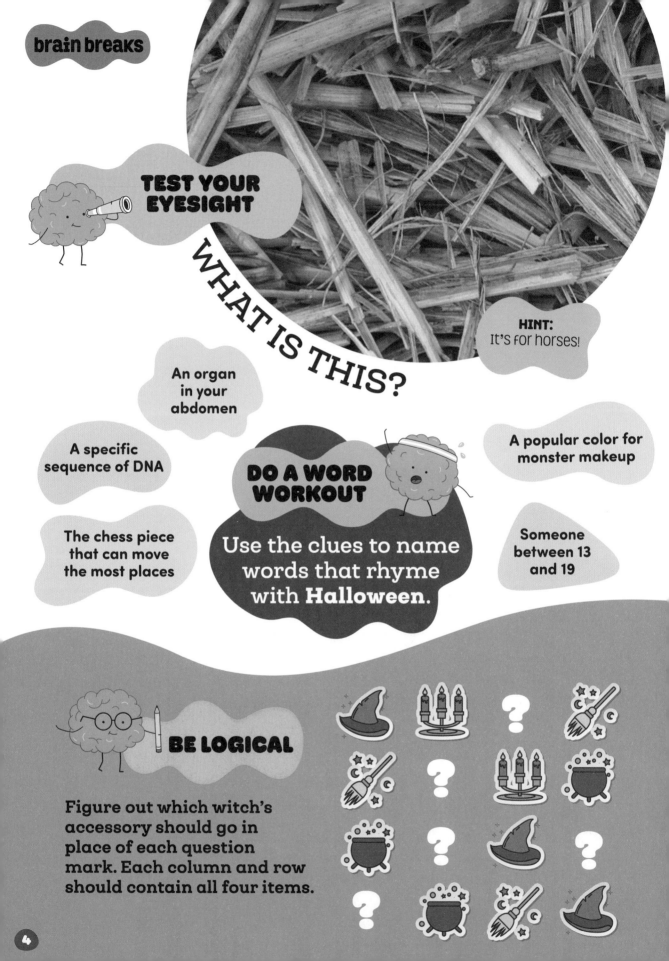

STRETCH YOUR MATH SKILLS

Franky Stine is making invitations for his upcoming Halloween party. He's inviting everyone from the spirit squad and engineering club. Using the clues, can you figure out how many invitations he'll give out?

1 Three of his friends are in both groups.

2 Including Franky, there are eight kids in the engineering club.

3 Six kids are in the spirit squad, not counting Franky.

THINK ABOUT IT

How would you describe a pumpkin without using the words *orange* or *fall*?

What would fit inside a pumpkin?

Where would you be surprised to see a pumpkin?

TICKLE YOUR FUNNY BONE

Knock, knock.
Who's there?
Fangs.
Fangs who?
Fangs for letting me in.

SCHOOL SPIRIT

FIND THESE OBJECTS IN THE SCENE.

arrow
artist's brush
bat
bell
broccoli
butter knife

button
candy cane
candy corn
carrot
crescent moon
crown

drinking straw
envelope
fishhook
hockey stick
lightning bolt
paper airplane

peanut
pennant
ring
ruler
seashell
slice of cheese

slice of pizza
snake
sock
spoon
toothbrush
yo-yo

party CLUES

Yennifer invited three friends to a Halloween party. Using the clues, can you figure out which ghost made each dish and decorated each pumpkin?

	white	orange	green	purple	boo-berries	spooketti noodles	tomb-ato sauce	vanilla iscream
Yennifer								
Enid								
Shen								
Hugh								

Use the chart to keep track of your answers. Put an **X** in every box that can't be true and an **O** in boxes that are true.

PARTY CLUES

1 Shen picked his fruity treat right before he spilled the green paint he used on his pumpkin.

2 The ghost who decorated the white pumpkin brought a frozen dessert.

3 Hugh's pumpkin is the only one without a face.

4 Enid wouldn't reveal her secret sauce recipe to the ghost who made spooketti noodles.

MONSTERS at the MOVIES

The movie's about to start! Set a timer for two minutes and see if you can find these snacks in time!

7 drinks

8 ice-cream cones

9 bags of popcorn

A-MAZE-ING MAZES

Check out these maze facts (and puzzles) from across the USA!

CALIFORNIA

ARIZONA

PICK A PUMPKIN

With its 63-acre maze, Cool Patch Pumpkins in Dixon, California, set the Guinness World Record in 2014 for the biggest corn maze.

GUESS THE REAL PUMPKIN VARIETY IN EACH PAIR.

Hijinks or Shenanigans?

Super Star or Super Moon?

Mama Bear or Baby Bear?

Fairytale or Fantasy?

WTRMLN

CCMBRS

Autumn Gold or Fall Silver?

Charm or Charisma?

THEME QUIZ

Treinen Farm in Lodi, Wisconsin, creates a new theme for their 15-acre maze each year.

ONE OF THESE THEMES IS FALSE. WHICH ONE?

Gecko Tesselations   Cheese the Day

Water Bear Maze   Crane Dance Maze

Mermaze

WISCONSIN

TIC TAC TRACTOR

Connors Farm in Danvers, Massachusetts, has been operating since 1904.

What do the tractors in each row (up, across, and diagonally) have in common?

MASSACHUSETTS

WE'RE ALL EARS

Great Scott Farms in Mount Dora, Florida, sells sweet corn that comes in fresh from their fields.

CAN YOU FIND THE EAR OF CORN WITH NO MATCH?

FLORIDA

MISSING VOWELS

In addition to their 20-acre corn maze, Apple Annie's Orchard in Willcox, Arizona, also offers a variety of pick-your-own produce.

CAN YOU IDENTIFY THE NAME OF EACH CROP?

TMTS

GGPLNT   GRN BNS

That's batty!

Can you find the opossum? How about the 12 spiders?

FACE-OFF

Every creature should only appear once in each row, column, and 2 x 3 box. Fill in the squares by drawing or by writing the number of each picture.

Why wasn't Dr. Frankenstein ever lonely?

Because he was so good at making new friends.

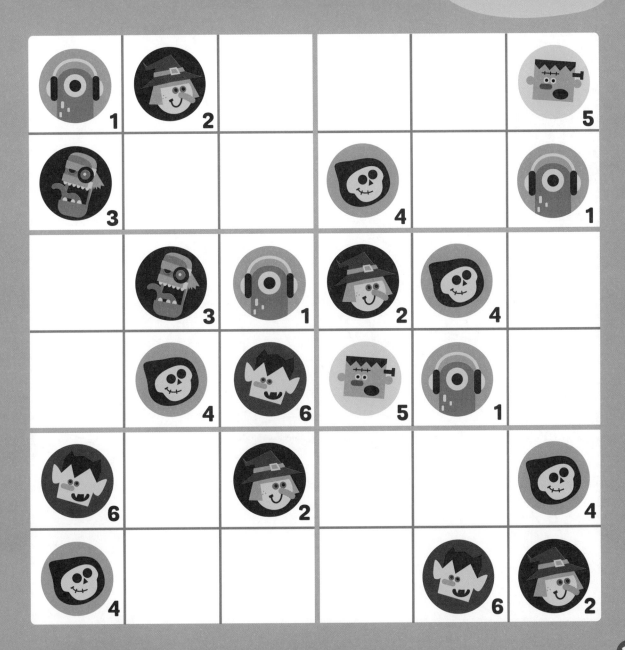

SQUISH SQUASH

Squash is one of the oldest-known crops. Some of the varieties are pictured here. Can you go from one end of the maze to the other? Begin at START and make your way to FINISH, passing through the numbers in order from 1 to 5 without backtracking or repeating any routes.

FUN FACT!

The word *squash* comes from *asquutasquash*, the Narragansett tribe's word for "raw" or "uncooked." Today, most squash is served cooked. What's your favorite way to eat squash?

 END

FUNNY Fall Fest

Which things in this picture are silly? It's up to you!

Math MIRTH

Do some math, then get a laugh!
Use the fractions of the words listed
below to solve the riddles.

what do ghosts put on their bagels?

_ _ _ _ _ _ _

_ _ _ _ _ _ _ _ .

First 1/3 of **SCENIC**
Middle 1/2 of **CREW**
Last 1/2 of **GLAM**

First 3/4 of **CHEW**
Last 3/5 of **THESE**

where do ghosts like to go for dinner?

_ _ _ _ _ _ _ _ _ _ _ _ _

_ _ _ _ _ _ .

First 3/4 of **TOAD**
Last 1/2 of **FIRE**
First 1/2 of **STARRY**

First 1/5 of **UNDER**
Middle 1/2 of **WHAT**
Last 3/4 of **AUNT**

what do ghosts eat for lunch?

_ _ _ _ _ _ - _ _ _ .

Last 1/3 of **JIG**
First 2/5 of **HOWDY**

Middle 1/2 of **GULP**
Last 3/4 of **WASH**

17

A FRESH SET OF
Eyes

Each cookie has an exact match—except for one.
Can you find the one without a match?

Monster Movie

Find 25 differences between the two pages.

Can you also find these details in the picture below?

Merry Monsters

mitten

comb

ladybug

?
question
mark

toothbrush

E
letter *E*

fork

pair of
pants

pea
pod

crown

gift

pennant

hat

spoon

teacup

sock

worm

BONUS!
Can you also find
the fish, pencil,
slice of pizza, and
ice-cream cone?

what's COOKING?

The 13 words below are different ways of describing what might be bubbling in a witch's cauldron. Each word will fit into the grid in only one way. Once you fill them in, unscramble the highlighted letters to find the answer to the riddle.

HINT: use the number of letters in each word as a clue to where it might fit.

O O Z E

WORD LIST

BREW
CONCOCTION
DRAFT
ELIXIR
GOO
GUNK
MIXTURE
~~OOZE~~
POTION

SLIME
SLUDGE
STEW
TONIC

what is a witch's favorite subject?

_ _ _ _ _ _ _ _ _ _ .

23

TEST YOUR EYESIGHT

WHAT IS THIS?

This performer doesn't need any words

HINT: watch your teeth!

DO A WORD WORKOUT

Use the clues to name words that rhyme with **SLIME**.

This puzzle is full of them

A musical sound

A coin

An aromatic herb

To rise or ascend

STRETCH YOUR MATH SKILLS

Each jack-o'-lantern represents a number. Look at the equations to figure out which number each jack-o'-lantern represents.

$1 + 4 = $ 🎃

🎃 $+$ 🎃 $=$ 🎃

🎃 $+$ 🎃 $=$ 🎃

BE LOGICAL

How can you make three cuts on this cake to get eight pieces?

STRETCH YOUR MIND

How many types of apples can you name in **ONE MINUTE?**

TICKLE YOUR FUNNY BONE

HA HA !!

What do you call a pumpkin comedian?

A joke-o'-lantern.

🎃 + 🎃 = 15

🎃 − 🎃 = 2

25

WITCH CRAFTS

FIND THESE OBJECTS IN THE SCENE.

arrow
baseball bat
bell
bottle
button
comb

domino
envelope
fish
fork
horseshoe
key

ladder
ladle
magnifying glass
mitten
necklace
nail

necktie
paper airplane
paper clip
rolling pin
ruler
slice of pizza

snail
sock
spool of thread
tennis racket
toothbrush
tube of toothpaste

Halloween WHO'S WHO

Four cousins are making their Halloween costumes together. Anna, Justin, Cathleen, and Pedro will each wear a different costume. One cousin will dress as a ghost, one as a superhero, one as a scarecrow, and one as a robot. Use the clues to figure out which costume each cousin will wear.

Use the chart to keep track of your answers. Put an **X** in every box that can't be true and an **O** in boxes that are true.

	ghost	superhero	scarecrow	robot
Anna				
Justin				
cathleen				
pedro				

CLUES

1 The cousin who will wear a cape is not a boy.

2 Anna will put on gray face paint to match her costume.

3 Justin will not use hay to stuff his costume.

4 The cousin who will wear a white sheet is not a girl.

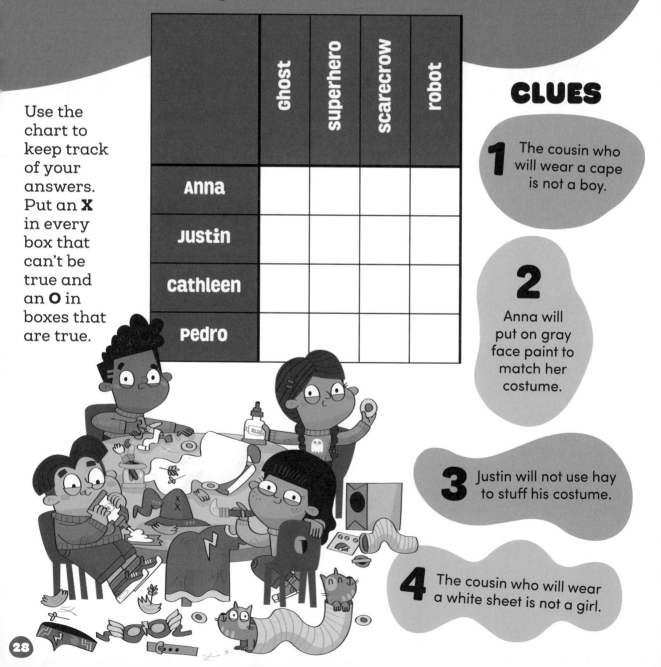

TAKE IT OR LEAF IT

Start at each blank leaf and follow its branch to the trunk. Can you find:

1 The branch that has only odd-numbered leaves?

2 The branch with leaves that add up to exactly 19?

3 The branch with leaves that add up to the lowest score?

4 The branch with leaves that add up to the highest score of any branch?

29

LET'S PARTY!

Check out these Halloween facts—and puzzles—from across the USA!

VNSHNG VWLS

The first U.S. Halloween was celebrated in Anoka, Minnesota, which is now known as the "Halloween Capital of the World." **CAN YOU UNMASK THESE SPOOKY WORDS?**

CNDY **SPKY** **TRCK-R-TRT**

MSK

CSTM

HAWAI'I

SEEK AND TREAT

In a twist on trick-or-treating, Kailua Town, Hawai'i, hosts an event in which *keiki* (kids) solve riddles and puzzles in order to earn a treat. The five locations families travel to have fun names, like The Forbidden Tree or The Broken Wand.

FIND 5 DIFFERENCES BETWEEN THESE BUCKETS.

CAL C. UHM

IKE N. FLY

HUGO FIRST

D. COMPOSING

YOU DON'T KNOW JACK-O'-LANTERNS

Hallowe'en in Greenfield Village, Michigan, is a month-long festival that features an illuminated path with over a thousand jack-o'-lanterns.

WHICH VEGETABLE WAS **NOT** CARVED TO MAKE JACK-O'-LANTERNS IN THE 19TH CENTURY?

turnip

bell pepper

beet

potato

MINNESOTA

MICHIGAN

NEW YORK

LOUISIANA

PARADE MAZE

Manhattan's annual Greenwich Village Halloween Parade is the largest Halloween parade in the world. **Help the monsters find the quickest path downtown to the parade.**

START

BOOKS NEVER WRITTEN

New Orleans, Louisiana, is one of America's most haunted cities. People can celebrate Halloween in New Orleans by exploring cemeteries or taking haunted tours.

CAN YOU MATCH THE "AUTHOR" OF EACH BOOK TO THE TITLE?

A Guide to Broomsticks

An Encyclopedia of Zombies

Into the Haunted House

Skeleton Bones

END

Tasty Treats

Every cupcake should only appear once in each row, column, and 2 x 3 box. Fill in the squares by drawing or by writing the number of each picture.

Say this tongue twister three times fast! Spooky cooks cook quirky cupcakes.

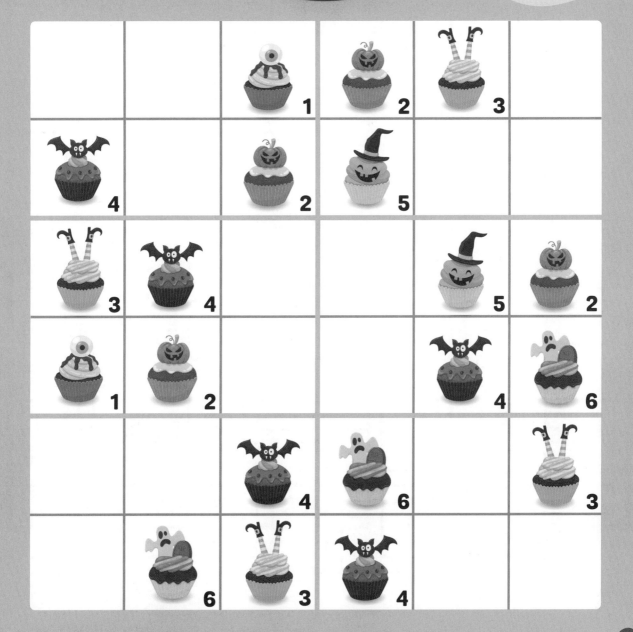

maze

watch out for MONSTERS!

SNACK SHACK

START

34

This haunted maze is full of monsters. Can you find a way through the maze without passing through any of the monsters? Start at the **ENTRANCE** on page 34 and find the path to the **SNACK SHACK**. Then start at the **SNACK SHACK** on page 35 and find your way to the exit.

SNACK SHACK

END

COSTUME CHAOS

Which things in this picture
are silly? It's up to you!

Rearranging
the artwork

To read the jumbled message, move the letters from each column into the boxes directly above them while staying in the same row. But watch out: the letters do not always go in the boxes in the same order as they appear. Each letter is used only once. We've filled in some to get you started. Roll up your sleeves, and get to work!

candy cone

There are 18 traffic cones
hiding among the candy corn.
Can you find them all?

DO A WORD WORKOUT

Use the clues to name words that can be made from the letters in **MELLOWCREME.**
(Did you know that's what candy corn is made from?)

The sound a cat makes

The master of ceremonies

A tiny burrowing creature

A group of people working together

The opposite of *higher*

Trick or Tweet

Find 23 differences between the two pages.

STRETCH YOUR MATH SKILLS

Mandy's change

Mandy used her pocket change to buy a caramel-swirl chocolate bar that cost $1.08. Afterward, she had one coin left. Which coin was it?

getting in the spirit!

 ladder

 ring

 hatchet

fish

BONUS!
Can you also find the house, heart, paper clip, ruler, and artist's brush?

fishhook

wedge of lemon

comb

teacup

pea pod

slice of bread

bowling ball

button

crown

slice of pizza

 crescent moon

 bell

pennant

LETTER DROP

Only six of the letters in the top line will work their way through this maze to land in the numbered squares at the bottom. When they get there, they will spell out the answer to the riddle.

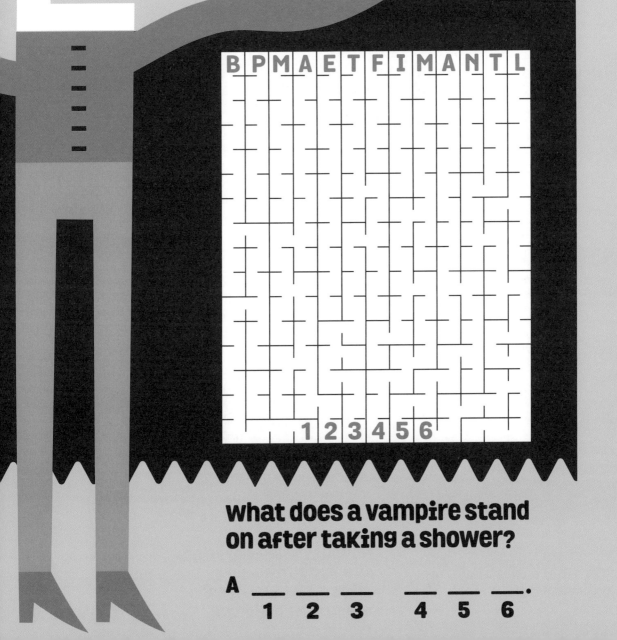

B P M A E T F I M A N T L

1 2 3 4 5 6

what does a vampire stand on after taking a shower?

A __ __ __ __ __ __.
  1 2 3   4 5 6

TICKLE YOUR FUNNY BONE

HA HA HA !!

What is a ghost's favorite position in soccer?

Ghoul-keeper.

DO A WORD WORKOUT

Are each of these spooky expressions **true** or **false**?

A GHOST TOWN is bustling with people.

Someone who's a NIGHT OWL likes being up late.

Someone who works the GRAVEYARD SHIFT works 9–5.

If something MAKES YOUR BLOOD BOIL, you're super annoyed.

If you SPILL YOUR GUTS, you need a bandage immediately.

BE LOGICAL

Can you figure out where all this would be true?

Day of the Dead, then Halloween;
candy, then costume.
A broomstick appears before a witch,
And gravestone before tomb.

Frivolity soon after fright,
First scream, and then comes yawn.
Tricks right after treats,
And night after dawn.

STRETCH YOUR MATH SKILLS

The total costs of the candy in each row and column is given. **Can you figure out the price of each group of candy?**

			$5.60
			$4.80
			$3.60
$4.40	$5.20	$4.40	

THINK ABOUT IT

Why does candy come in different colors?

Do you think animals eat dessert?

If you could invent a new candy bar, what would it be called?

WHAT IS THIS?

TEST YOUR EYESIGHT

C AND Y FACTORY

FIND THESE OBJECTS IN THE SCENE.

belt
canoe
comb
crown
envelope
flyswatter

hairbrush
hammer
hockey stick
ice-cream cone
ice-cream scooper
key

kite
magnet
magnifying glass
nail
pencil
pennant

ring
ruler
sailboat
saltshaker
saucepan
screwdriver

shovel
skateboard
sock
sunglasses
yo-yo

It's always
Chews-day at
the C and Y Factory

Road Trip on Planet Slime

On Planet Slime, color rules! To travel around, you must leave any purple house by a road that's a different color from the one you came in on. How many moves will it take you to get from START to FINISH?

start

Finish

BONUS!

Are there more green, yellow, or pink artist's brushes hidden in this picture?

A MOONLIT CODE

Just like the sun, the moon rises in the east and sets in the west. To answer the riddle below, start at the EAST (E) circle. Then move in the directions listed and write the letters you find in the correct spaces. Get cracking before the moon sets and it's time for the owl to go to bed!

N

```
Q   E   A   M   B
F   O   D   Y   I
N   S   J   E   H
G   O   P   R   W
L   K   C   P   W
```

W

E

S

what do owls say when they go trick-or-treating?

1. W 1 _____

2. NW 2 _____

3. S 3 _____

4. SE 1 _____

5. N 3 _____

6. W 2 _____

7. SE 3 _____

8. W 4 _____

9. NE 1 _____

10. E 3 _____

11. NW 3 _____

12. SE 2 _____

13. W 3 _____

49

WHICH WAY USA

TERRIFYING TOWN NAMES

Check out these spooky-town facts—and puzzles—from across the USA!

FRANKEN-PUZZLE

No monsters here! Frankenstein, Missouri, was named after Godfried Franken, who donated land to the town in 1890.

THE DEVIL'S IN THE DETAILS

Red Devil, Alaska, was named after a nearby (now abandoned) mine, which got its name from the toxic red ore found there.

ARE EACH OF THESE RED EXPRESSIONS TRUE OR FALSE?

IF YOU PLAN TO **PAINT THE TOWN RED**, YOU'RE GOING TO NEED PAINTBRUSHES.

A **RED FLAG** IS NOT SOMETHING TO IGNORE.

SOMEONE WHO GOT CAUGHT **RED-HANDED** IS GOING TO BE IN TROUBLE.

A **RED-LETTER DAY** IS A SUPER BORING DAY.

SPELLING ERROR

Casper, Wyoming, was named after Fort Caspar, which was named after Lieutenant Caspar Collins. But someone made a mistake when the town's name was officially registered, and CaspAr became CaspEr. No relation to the famous ghost, unfortunately.

COME UP WITH AT LEAST 13 WORDS FROM THE LETTERS IN

FRIENDLY GHOST

FIND 5 DIFFERENCES BETWEEN THESE MONSTERS.

ODD BAT OUT

Bat Cave, North Carolina, is named after ... wait for it ... a nearby bat cave!

CAN YOU FIND THE BAT WITH NO MATCH?

MISSOURI

NORTH CAROLINA

TEXAS

WHERE'D EVERYBODY GO?

Texas has over 500 ghost towns—more than any other state—including Bitter Creek, Rath City, and Terlingua ("Three Tongues").

DRAW YOUR OWN GHOST TOWN HERE.

candy con

Can you find the carrot?
How about the 12
gummy worms?

SO MONSTER-iOUS

Every monster should only appear once in each row, column, and 2 x 3 box. Fill in the squares by drawing or by writing the number of each picture.

What's the best way to talk to a monster?

Long distance.

A-MAZE-ING CORN

Make your way from START to FINISH through the corn maze. Once you've found the right path, write the letters along it in order in the spaces below to answer the riddle.

what did the corn maze say when the scarecrow gave it a compliment?

" A __ __ , __ __ __ __ __ __ __ ,

__ __ __ __ __ __ __ ! "

F
H
N
S
A
K
D
S
END
A
START
R
T
W

what's wrong?

HAUNTED HIJINKS

Which things in this picture are silly? It's up to you!

Can you also find 10 hidden bananas?

vampire cross-out

To get the answer to the riddle below, first cross out all the pairs of matching letters. Then write the remaining letters in order in the spaces below the riddle.

QQ	BB	EE	TO
LL	OO	WW	HH
IM	YY	DD	PP
UU	AA	LL	HH
DD	XX	PR	GG
ZZ	OV	OO	TT
SS	CC	EH	II
CC	DD	IS	MM
AA	TT	BB	JJ
AA	RR	FF	BI
EE	YY	KK	TE
NN	VV	ZZ	QQ
CC	UU	BB	SS

why did the vampire go to the dentist?

_ _ _ _ _ _ _ _ _ _ _ _

_ _ _ _ _ _ _ _.

BONUS!

Can you find 16 hidden objects in the scene?

57

C

B

A

D

plenty of
Pumpkins

Can you find these **8 jigsaw pieces**
in this photo of pumpkins?

E

F

G

H

PUNKIN' CHUNKIN'

Find 26 differences between the two pages.

Did You Know?

Kids ten and under can compete, too! In the youth category, the current record holders are:

Pumpkin Pirates' trebuchet (550.43 ft)

Little Blasters (1,939.81 ft)

Jersey Devil's catapult (1,272.64 ft)

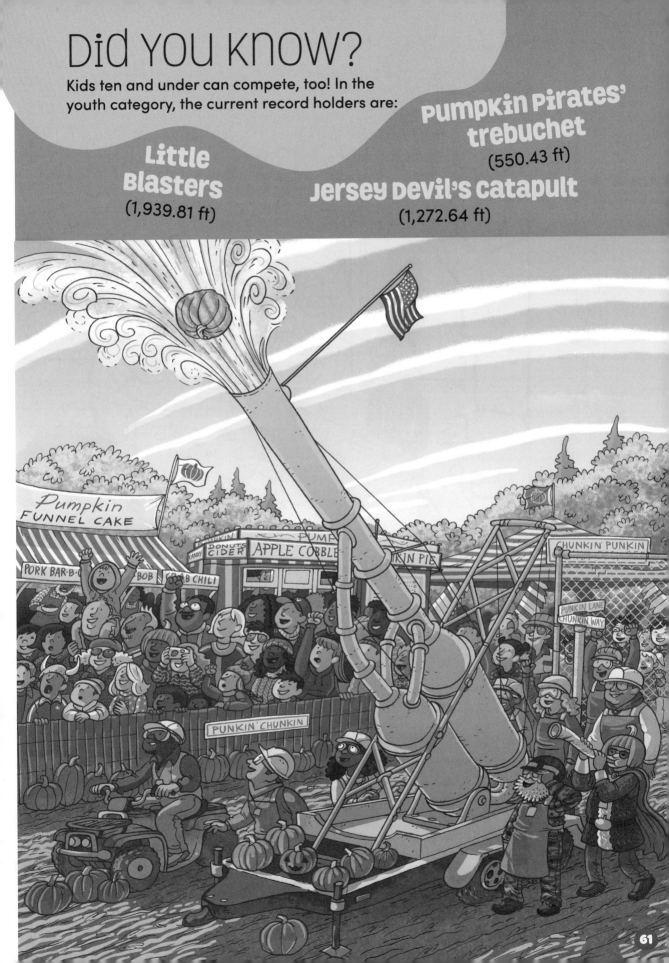

crown

pepper

waffle

lightning bolt

drumstick

hockey stick

monster mash

adhesive bandage

domino

bell

thumbtack

broccoli

ruler

WORD FOR WORDS

The letters in **MONSTER MOVIE** can be used to make many other words. Use the clues below to come up with some of them.

MONSTER MOVIE

1. The number of continents

___ ___ ___ ___ ___

2. Worn under a suit jacket

___ ___ ___ ___ ___

3. A person who works underground

___ ___ ___ ___ ___

4. Use this to change the channel

___ ___ ___ ___ ___ ___

5. The opposite of silence

___ ___ ___ ___ ___

6. A funny cat picture

___ ___ ___ ___

7. A small piece of rock

___ ___ ___ ___ ___

63

THINK ABOUT IT

CAN YOU RUN FASTER WITH YOUR HANDS IN OR OUT OF YOUR POCKETS? WHY?

what's the last thing you made by hand?

WHAT DO PEOPLE DO WITH THEIR HANDS WHEN THEY FEEL SCARED? NERVOUS? EXCITED?

TEST YOUR EYESIGHT

WHAT IS THIS?

SAY THIS THREE TIMES FAST:

Plump pumpkin guts plopped on the patio.

HINT: scoop it out!

STRETCH YOUR MATH SKILLS

Use the clues to figure out the address of Mr. E's haunted house.

The house number ends with a multiple of 3.

The address has at least one letter that comes after *W* in the alphabet.

Its numerals add up to an even number.

1313
Broomstick
Boulevard

666
Graveyard
Road

3131
Spooky Lane

DO A WORD WORKOUT

Use the clues to name words that contain **BAT.**

A conductor uses one

A fluffy garment that wraps around you

Money you get back

A heated argument

It provides power

BE LOGICAL

TRICK OR TREAT

BOO

Jayanthi and her cousin Ishan both plan to go trick-or-treating at 5:00 P.M. Jayanthi will start two hours before Ishan. **HOW CAN THIS BE?**

TICKLE YOUR FUNNY BONE

HA HA !!

Knock, knock.
Who's there?
Ghost.
Ghost who?
Ghost to show you don't remember my name!

FA-BOO-LOUS!

FIND THESE OBJECTS IN THE SCENE.

artist's brush	broom	fried egg	magician's wand	pencil
banana	crescent moon	golf club	mitten	pennant
baseball	doughnut	harmonica	muffin	ruler
book	drinking straw	kite	needle	sock
boomerang	envelope	lollipop	paper clip	yo-yo

KITTY Lit

These cats love the library! Using the clues, can you figure out how many books in which genre each cat checked out?

	Horror	Comedy	Fantasy	History	2	4	6	8
Count Catula								
Vampurra								
Clawsper								
Tabbytha								

Use the chart to keep track of your answers. Put an **X** in every box that can't be true and an **O** in boxes that are true.

CLUES

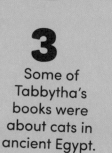

1 Count Catula checked out twice as many books as Clawsper and six more than Vampurra.

2 Vampurra showed her scary books to the cat whose four books were about mermaids, unicorns, dragons, and gnomes.

3 Some of Tabbytha's books were about cats in ancient Egypt.

spooky SCOOPS

Each coded space has two numbers. The first number tells you which flavor to look at; the second number tells you which letter in that flavor to use.

1. VEINILLA
2. DEATH BY CHOCOLATE
3. ROCKY ROADKILL
4. COOKIES AND SCREAM
5. KEY SLIME PIE
6. COBWEB CANDY
7. MINT SHOCKLATE CHIP
8. BRAINBOW SHERBERT
9. FRUIT AND GUTS

What do ghosts put on their sundaes?

___ ___ ___ ___ ___ ___ ___
6-4   2-5   3-11   5-9   7-17   1-2   6-10

___ ___ ___ ___ ___ ___ .
4-7   7-14   8-2   5-8   1-8   4-16

How does a scarecrow drink a milkshake?

___ ___ ___ ___   ___
8-8   5-6   9-5   7-6   2-3

___ ___ ___ ___ ___ .
4-11   7-4   8-2   3-8   6-4

What do zombies say when you offer them ice cream?

"
___ ___
4-3   9-1

___ ___ ___ ___ ___ ___ !"
2-8   8-7   3-6   5-9   9-12   1-2

BONUS!
Each spooky sundae uses one flavor of ice cream plus one topping. If the ice-cream shop offers three different toppings, how many unique sundaes can you make?

answers

COVER

BRAIN WARMUPS

pages 4–5

TEST YOUR EYESIGHT: a pile of hay
DO A WORD WORKOUT: spleen, gene, queen, green, teen
BE LOGICAL:

STRETCH YOUR MATH SKILLS: Franky gives out nine invitations.

SCHOOL SPIRIT

pages 6–7

PARTY CLUES

page 8

YENNIFER: purple; spooketti noddles
ENID: orange; tomb-ato sauce
SHEN: green; boo-berries
HUGH: white; vanilla iscream

MONSTERS AT THE MOVIES

page 9

A-MAZE-ING MAZES

pages 10–11

PICK A PUMPKIN: Hijinks, Baby Bear, Super Moon, Fairytale, Autumn Gold, Charisma
THEME QUIZ: Mermaze
WE'RE ALL EARS:

TIC TAC TRACTOR:

yellow vintage-style hay bales	vintage-style trailer	vintage-style smoke red hubcaps
yellow roof	roof hay bales red hubcaps trailer	smoke roof
yellow bucket red hubcaps	trailer bucket	smoke hay bales bucket

MISSING VOWELS: cucumbers, watermelon, tomatoes, eggplant, green beans

THAT'S BATTY!

page 12

SQUISH SQUASH

pages 14–15

A FRESH SET OF EYES

pages 18–19

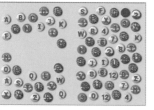

FACE-OFF

page 13

MATH MIRTH

page 17

WHAT DO GHOSTS PUT ON THEIR BAGELS?
SCREAM CHEESE.
WHERE DO GHOSTS LIKE TO GO FOR DINNER?
TO A RESTAU-HAUNT.
WHAT DO GHOSTS EAT FOR LUNCH?
GHOUL-ASH.

MONSTER MOVIE

pages 20–21

MERRY MONSTERS

page 22

WHAT'S COOKING?

page 23

WHAT IS A WITCH'S FAVORITE SUBJECT?
SPELLING.

BRAIN BREAKS

pages 24–25

TEST YOUR EYESIGHT: a candy apple
DO A WORD WORKOUT: mime, rhyme, dime, thyme, climb, chime
STRETCH YOUR MATH SKILLS:

= 5   = 3   = 10   =7

BE LOGICAL: Make two cuts top to bottom across the cake, creating four pieces. Then slice horizontally through the middle of the cake, cutting though four pieces to make eight pieces.

WITCH CRAFTS

pages 26–27

HALLOWEEN WHO'S WHO

page 28

ANNA: robot
JUSTIN: ghost
CATHLEEN: superhero
PEDRO: scarecrow

TAKE IT OR LEAF IT

page 29

How do you make a witch itch?

TAKE AWAY THE W.

answers

LET'S PARTY!

pages 30–31

SEEK AND TREAT: VANISHING VOWELS: candy, spooky, trick-or-treat, mask, costume

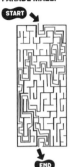

YOU DON'T KNOW JACK-O'-LANTERNS: bell pepper
PARADE MAZE:

BOOKS NEVER WRITTEN:
A Guide to Broomsticks by Ike N. Fly
An Encyclopedia of Zombies by D. Composing
Into the Haunted House by Hugo First
Skeleton Bones by Cal C. Uhm

WHOOO'S THERE?

page 32

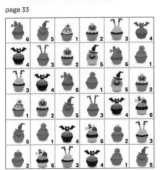

TASTY TREATS

page 33

WATCH OUT FOR MONSTERS!

pages 34–35

REARRANGING THE ARTWORK

page 37

WHAT IS A WITCH'S FAVORITE HOBBY? ARTS AND WITCHCRAFTS

TRICK OR TWEET

pages 40–41

STRETCH YOUR MATH SKILLS: Mandy had one quarter left over.

LETTER DROP

page 43

WHAT DOES A VAMPIRE STAND ON AFTER TAKING A SHOWER? A BAT MAT.

CANDY CONE

pages 38–39

DO A WORD WORKOUT: meow, emcee, mole, crew, lower

GETTING IN THE SPIRIT!

page 42

BRAIN BREAKS

pages 44–45

DO A WORD WORKOUT:
GHOST TOWN: false
MAKES YOUR BLOOD BOIL: true
SPILL YOUR GUTS: false
GRAVEYARD SHIFT: false
NIGHT OWL: true
BE LOGICAL: In the dictionary
STRETCH YOUR MATH SKILLS:

$2.00 $1.20 $1.60

TEST YOUR EYESIGHT: gummy worms

C AND Y FACTORY

pages 46–47

ROAD TRIP ON PLANET SLIME

page 48

We made it to the FINISH in six moves; perhaps you found another route.
BONUS: There are six pink artist's brushes, five green artist's brushes, and four orange artist's brushes.

A MOONLIT CODE

page 49

WHAT DO OWLS SAY WHEN THEY GO TRICK-OR-TREATING? "HAPPY OWL-O-WEEN!"

What kind of candy is never on time?
CHOCO-LATE.

answers

TERRIFYING TOWN NAMES

pages 50–51

THE DEVIL'S IN THE DETAILS:
PAINT THE TOWN RED: false
RED FLAG: true
RED-HANDED: true
RED-LETTER DAY: false

SPELLING ERROR: We came up with these words. You may have thought of others. Fig, fly, got, hen, her, hey, hid, hot, leg, net, nor, old, red, shy, try, dine, dire, felt, fist, foil, fort, gold, golf, life, nose, rein, rest, shoe, sigh, soil, yeti, diner, dinghy, dirty, forty, heist

FRANKEN-PUZZLE: **ODD BAT OUT:**

CANDY CON

page 52

SO MONSTER-IOUS

page 53

A-MAZE-ING CORN

pages 54–55

WHAT DID THE CORN MAZE SAY WHEN THE SCARECROW GAVE IT A COMPLIMENT?
"AW, SHUCKS, THANKS!"

HAUNTED HIJINKS

page 56

VAMPIRE CROSS-OUT

page 57

WHY DID THE VAMPIRE GO TO THE DENTIST? TO IMPROVE HIS BITE.

PLENTY OF PUMPKINS

pages 58–59

PUNKIN' CHUNKIN'

pages 60–61

MONSTER MASH

page 62

WORD FOR WORDS

page 63

1. seven
2. vest
3. miner
4. remote
5. noise
6. meme
7. stone

BRAIN BREAKS

pages 64–65

TEST YOUR EYESIGHT: pumpkin guts
STRETCH YOUR MATH SKILLS: Mr. E's address is 666 Graveyard Road.
DO A WORD WORKOUT: baton, bathrobe, rebate, debate, battery
BE LOGICAL: Jayanthi lives two time zones ahead of Ishan. When it is 5:00 P.M. where Jayanthi lives, it is only 3:00 P.M. where Ishan lives.

FA-BOO-LOUS!

pages 66–67

KITTY LIT

page 68

COUNT CATULA: comedy; 8
VAMPURRA: horror; 2
CLAWSPER: fantasy; 4
TABBYTHA: history; 6

SPOOKY SCOOPS

page 69

WHAT DO GHOSTS PUT ON THEIR SUNDAES?
WHIPPED SCREAM.
HOW DOES A SCARECROW DRINK A MILKSHAKE?
WITH A STRAW.
WHAT DO ZOMBIES SAY WHEN YOU OFFER THEM ICE CREAM?
"OF CORPSE!"
BONUS: You can make 3 different sundaes with each flavor. There are 9 flavors. So the answer is 9 x 3, or 27 sundaes.

BACK COVER

COVER ART by Jana Curll

TEXT CREDITS: Teresa A. DiNicola (28); Marianne Murphy (2–3); James Vorosmarti (48)

PHOTO AND ILLUSTRATION CREDITS:
David Arumi (57); Beccy Blake (9); Iryna Bodnaruk (26–27); Elizabeth Carpenter (14–15); Daryll Collins (6–7, 20–21, 66–67); Jana Curll (32, 52); Chuck Dillon (60–61); Joey Ellis (48); Travis Foster (12); Getty Images (4–5, 8, 10–11, 13, 17, 18–19, 23, 24–25, 30–31, 33, 34–35, 37, 38–39, 43, 44–45, 49, 50–51, 53, 58–59, 63, 64–65, 68, 69); Bill Golliher (38–39); Kelly Kennedy (46–47, 56); Dave Klug (54–55); Gary LaCoste (2–3); James Loram (51); Mitch Mortimer (16); Gina Perry (22, 42); Dave Phillips (34–35); Kevin Rechin (44); Jaka Vukotič (29); Brian Michael Weaver (11, 40–41, 62); Dave Whamond (36); Steven Wood (28)

For information about permission to reprint selections from this book, please contact permissions@highlights.com.

Published by Highlights Press
815 Church Street
Honesdale, Pennsylvania 18431
ISBN: 978-1-63962-251-1
Manufactured in
Dongguan City, Guangdong, China
Mfg. 03/2024

First edition
Visit our website at Highlights.com.
10 9 8 7 6 5 4 3 2 1